HUKA LODGE

Consistently listed amongst
the top retreats of the world.

Recipes by
NICHOLAS WATT

Recipe photographs by
NICK TRESIDDER

EDITORS: Diana Harris, Lauraine Jacobs and Barbara Nielsen
ART DIRECTION AND STYLING: Donna Hoyle
PHOTOGRAPHY: Recipes Nick Tresidder; all other photographs by Geoff Mason
DESIGN: Donna Hoyle and Michael Wrightson
TYPESETTING: Claire O'Connor Graphic Studio
PRE-PRESS: Spectra Graphics
PRINTING AND BINDING: Everbest Printing Co. Ltd
DINNERWARE FOR PHOTOGRAPHY: The Studio of Tableware

Published by Huka Lodge
P.O. Box 95, Taupo, New Zealand

Copyright © 2003 Huka Lodge
Nicholas Watt (recipes), Nick Tresidder
and Geoff Mason (photographs)

First published 2003
Reprinted 2004
ISBN 0-473-09955-1

HUKA LODGE

*Consistently listed amongst
the top retreats of the world.*

Chef's
Secrets

RECIPES FROM THE HUKA LODGE KITCHEN

CONTENTS

INTRODUCTION

by Alex van Heeren

It was in 1984 when my wife, Anne Marie, and I first drove through the gates, down the drive, turned the bend and caught sight of Huka Lodge.

The hypnotic and dangerous force of the powerful Waikato River with its intense turquoise hue was palpable as it swept downstream to the mighty Huka Falls. The magnificent views were framed by the mature trees on the river banks.

This was truly a special place worthy of preserving – it was love at first sight.

Early photographs soon revealed the Lodge's humble beginnings, where anglers were accommodated in simple huts with slatted floors and stout wooden frames draped with heavy canvas. The rustic arrangements were more than compensated for by the warmth and generosity of the original owner, Alan Pye, and his wife, Leila, back at the main lodge where drinks and hearty meals were the order of the day. Alan Pye was also something of a raconteur who encouraged guests to share their experiences and adventures.

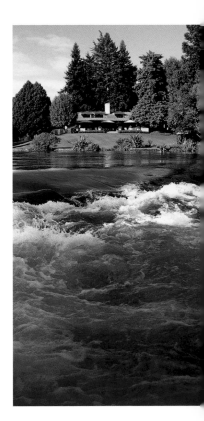

Alan Pye

Word soon spread about Huka Lodge, its hospitality and the most exciting trout fishing to be had in the area. By the mid-1930s, Alan Pye's fame was reaching a peak. Trout fishing flies were named after him and the Huka Lodge Guest Book included the names of many dignitaries and celebrities.

Despite the onset of World War II, Alan Pye's loyal guests still continued to come to Huka Lodge, and the emphasis moved to Lake Taupo and its tributaries.

Alan Pye died in 1973 leaving a legacy of personal hospitality, which has become a cornerstone of the present Huka Lodge.

My goal has been to revive the earlier ambience of Huka Lodge and to extend this to include a level of comfort and luxury never previously experienced.

Assisted by a highly talented and dedicated team, we have transformed the property into the reality it is today, with solid and comforting rooms and a genteel atmosphere embracing natural fibres and warm soft lighting – the emphasis is on harmony and simplicity.

The seven-hectare grounds are park-like and have been enriched by extensive plantings that blend seamlessly into the bordering Wairakei Park Reserve.

I like to think that Alan Pye would approve of Huka Lodge today. While blazing log fires are still a feature, they are now supplemented by stunning outdoor fireplaces. We still uphold the tradition of communal dining, however, we also offer the most romantic venues tucked away in special corners all over the grounds. He would certainly approve of the underground wine cellar and dining room.

Recreational opportunities abound – from mountain biking, golf, fly fishing, white and black water rafting, horse trekking, guided flora and fauna walks, helicopter sightseeing, and aquatic adventures on Lake Taupo, to our premier excursions, 'The White Island Experience' and 'The Huka Lodge Experience'.

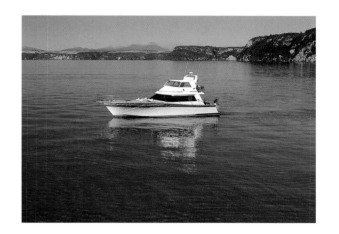

Fine dining is renowned at Huka Lodge, with hearty breakfasts, extensive tasty lunches and superb five-course dinners. As always, guests make their way from just twenty guest suites, all enjoying views of the river, down the path to the main lodge for pre-dinner drinks and dinner.

It is from these meals that Nicholas Watt, our executive chef, has selected a range of recipes and culinary secrets that we would like to share with you in this, our latest publication.

Nicholas has adapted the recipes for easy re-creation in your home for family and friends to enjoy – I am confident you will find them every bit as delicious as our guests do.

As caretaker of Huka Lodge and its legacy of gracious hospitality and warmth, I like to think that our solicitous attentiveness to all our guests and visitors is as palpable as the force of the old Waikato River.

Alex van Heeren
Owner, Huka Lodge

BIRCHER MUESLI, TOASTED ALMONDS AND GREEK YOGHURT

SERVES 4

180g rolled oats
350ml apple juice
8 tbsp Greek yoghurt
1 red Gala apple, grated
1 banana, sliced
4 tbsp almonds, toasted
4 tbsp manuka honey
   (or any fragrant honey)
6 fresh mint tips
6 fresh basil tips

Mix together the oats and apple juice. Soak overnight.

TO SERVE
Mix the soaked oats with half of the Greek yoghurt, and all of the apple and banana. Spoon into bowls and top with the remaining yoghurt, toasted almonds, honey, mint and basil tips.

CRUMPETS WITH MANUKA HONEY, MASCARPONE AND SMOKED BACON

SERVES 4

Crumpets
½ cup full cream milk
½ tsp sugar
2g dried yeast
110g standard or cake flour
1 pinch salt
1 pinch bicarbonate of soda
150ml water

Topping
12 strips smoked rindless
   bacon
4 tbsp manuka honey
   (or any fragrant honey)
4 tbsp mascarpone

To make the crumpets, heat the milk to blood temperature or about 38–40°C. Stir in the sugar and yeast. Let the mixture stand in a warm place for about 10 minutes.

Sift the flour and salt into the milk to form a thick batter and mix until completely smooth. Cover and leave to prove in a warm spot for about 1 hour or until the mixture has doubled in size.

Mix the bicarbonate of soda with the water and mix into the batter.

Spoon into heated, greased blini pans, about half full. Cook only on one side and finish the tops under the grill.

TO SERVE
Cook the bacon to crisp strips or to taste, place over the heated crumpets and drizzle with honey and a spoonful of mascarpone.

BLOOD ORANGE AND TOMATO MARMALADE

MAKES 1 LITRE

500g blood oranges
375ml boiling water
600g tomatoes, skinned
    and deseeded
90g caster sugar

Halve the oranges and slice into 4mm-thick rings. Pour the boiling water over the oranges and allow to stand overnight.

Bring the oranges and the liquid to a simmer and cook at a moderate heat until the oranges are tender.

Cut the tomatoes into rough pieces and stir into the orange mixture with the sugar. Stir until the sugar has completely dissolved.

Cook until the marmalade holds a skin when a spoonful is put on a plate.

Pour into sterilised glass jars, cover and allow to set.

The quantities for this recipe depend on the amount of crab apple juice you extract. If you follow the correct sequence, you will have a beautiful jelly that can go with cheese and meats.

crab apples
1 muslin cloth
rosewater
caster sugar

CRAB APPLE AND ROSEWATER JELLY

Begin by removing the stems and blossoms from the crab apples. Halve the crab apples and remove the stones but leave the skin on as this gives the colour.

Place the crab apples in a saucepan and cover with water. Cook them until they are soft and beginning to form a pink mush.

Transfer the crab apples and liquid to a muslin cloth and hang in a ball so the crab apple juice can run out. Do not squeeze out the juice or the jelly will become cloudy. Leave to hang with a catching bowl underneath for 24 hours.

Measure the juice and, for every cup you have, add 2 drops of rosewater and $2/3$ cup of caster sugar. Bring this mixture to a steady boil, until it forms a skin on the back of a spoon.

Pour into sterilised glass jars, cover and allow to set.

GRANOLA CRUNCHY CLUSTERS

SERVES 10

4 cups rolled oats
1 cup wheatgerm
1 cup light brown sugar
1/2 cup demerara sugar
1/2 tsp ground mixed spice
1/2 tsp ground cinnamon
1 pinch salt
1/4 cup hazelnut oil
1/2 cup full cream milk
1 cup dates, halved
1/2 cup sliced dried peaches
1/2 cup pumpkin seeds
1/2 cup sunflower seeds
1/2 cup dried coconut flakes
1/2 cup dried banana chips

Mix together the oats, wheatgerm, sugars, spices and salt. Rub in the hazelnut oil and milk to form grainy clusters.

Bake at 150°C for 40–45 minutes, stirring every 10 minutes, until they become golden and are in small clusters. Allow to cool.

Mix in the dates, peaches, pumpkin seeds, sunflower seeds, coconut flakes and banana chips.

Store in an airtight container.

SMOKED COD HASH WITH A POACHED EGG, SALMON CAVIAR AND HOLLANDAISE

SERVES 4

Smoked cod hash
180g smoked cod
180g potato, cooked
    and crushed
2 tbsp Italian parsley leaves
1 tbsp grated lemon zest

4 free range eggs
1 cup baby spinach
4 tbsp hollandaise sauce
4 tbsp salmon caviar

Make the cod hash in advance. Flake the smoked cod into bite-sized pieces. Mix with the crushed potato, parsley leaves and zest, using the crushed potato as the binding agent. Form into 4 even cakes, ready to be cooked. These can be kept for up to 3 days in the refrigerator.

Poach the eggs in a deep pot with a little added white vinegar and salt. Letting the egg fall into the boiling water allows it to form a beautiful oval shape.

Cook the cod hash cakes on both sides until lightly golden, then finish in the oven to ensure they are hot all the way through.

TO SERVE
Arrange the washed baby spinach on the plates, followed by the cooked cod hash cake. Top with the poached egg. Drizzle a spoonful of hollandaise sauce over and around the egg, and garnish with some salmon caviar.

VENISON AND APPLE SAUSAGES

MAKES 12

500g venison leg meat,
    minced
125g pancetta, minced
220g apple
1 tsp ground cinnamon
1 pinch coarsely ground
    black pepper
1 pinch sea salt
1 metre natural sausage skin

Mix the venison and pancetta together.

Peel the apple and cut into small, pea-sized cubes. Sauté the apple until tender and add the ground cinnamon. Allow the apple to cool before mixing it into the mince. Season with the black pepper and salt.

Wash the natural skin inside and out. Thread it onto the nozzle of a sausage gun and tie a knot at the end. Fill the sausage gun with the sausage mixture. Fill the casing to the desired size and twist between each sausage.

TO SERVE
This is the base for our Huka Lodge breakfast, which we serve with sourdough toast, portobello mushrooms and slow-baked Roma tomatoes.

PORTOBELLO MUSHROOMS,
SAGE BUTTER CURLS AND SOFT-BOILED EGGS

SERVES 4

2 sheets puff pastry
8 small portobello mushrooms
100g unsalted butter
½ cup fresh sage, chopped
4 free range eggs

Cut the puff pastry into 4 even rectangles and place on a greased baking tray.

Take the centre core out of the mushrooms. (Try to pick mushrooms where the cap is still closed under, as these will still have all the mushroom spores in them, with all the flavour.)

Soften the butter and mix in the sage. Brush some butter over each piece of puff pastry. Allow the remaining butter to harden again.

Place 2 mushrooms on each piece of puff pastry, and a knob of butter on each mushroom. Bake for 14 minutes at 180°C.

Soft-boil the eggs, and peel away the eggshell, keeping the egg intact.

TO SERVE
Set the mushroom puff pastry down first, put the intact soft-boiled egg on top and with a butter knife make curls of sage butter to go on top of this. Just as you are about to serve them, carefully split the eggs, allowing some of the yolk to run out.

WATERMELON, ROSEWATER-MARINATED FETA AND PISTACHIO SALAD

SERVES 4

1 watermelon

Rosewater marinade
35ml rosewater
150ml Riesling verjuice
1 tsp pink peppercorns,
    crushed
100ml avocado oil

220g feta cheese, cut
    into cubes
¹/₂ cup pistachio nuts
¹/₄ cup mint leaves, picked
    over, stalks removed
¹/₄ cup basil leaves, picked
    over, stalks removed

Cut the watermelon into even, bite-sized pieces.

Make the rosewater marinade by mixing the rosewater, verjuice, pink peppercorns and avocado oil together. Place the feta cheese pieces in the marinade and leave for 2–3 hours.

Crush half of the pistachio nuts.

TO SERVE
Toss the marinated cheese, watermelon, crushed nuts, mint and basil leaves together in a large bowl and finish with the remaining pistachios, for a refreshing light salad.

Wine match: *Champagne or aged New Zealand sparkling wine. Light and refreshing with a hint of nuttiness.*

BLACK MISSION FIG, MOZZARELLA, PRESERVED LEMON AND PINE NUT SALAD

SERVES 4

8 Black Mission figs
I large ball fresh mozzarella
I preserved lemon
2 tbsp fresh lemon juice
2 tbsp aged balsamic vinegar
4 tbsp extra virgin olive oil
¼ cup pine nuts, roasted
½ cup fresh basil, sliced finely
½ cup fresh mint, sliced finely

Slice the figs and pull apart the mozzarella into small pieces. Slice the preserved lemon into small pieces. Mix with the lemon juice and extra virgin olive oil. Crush the pine nuts coarsely and combine with the fig mixture. Mix in the fresh herbs.

TO SERVE
Arrange on a large platter or individual serving plates.

Wine match: *Dry or medium-dry Riesling. Citrus flavours and high acidity, with some sweetness of figs. Try Clare Valley or Eden Valley (Australia), or New Zealand Riesling.*

This salad is equally successful using peaches or plums at their seasonal peak.

GRILLED NECTARINE, PROSCIUTTO CRUDO AND BOCCONCINI SALAD

SERVES 4

6 nectarines, stoned and
    quartered
12 slices prosciutto
12 bocconcini
2 cups watercress
1 bunch fresh coriander
2 tbsp fresh lemon juice
6 tbsp extra virgin olive oil
2 pinches sea salt
coarsely ground black pepper

Grill the nectarines so that the natural sugars caramelise and form grill markings, giving a lovely bittersweet mix. Let the fruit cool to room temperature.

Shred the prosciutto into small lengths and drain the cheese. Pick over the watercress and coriander, removing the stalks.

To make the dressing, mix the lemon juice, olive oil, salt and pepper.

TO SERVE
Build the salad in layers on the plate and then spoon the dressing over.

Wine match: *Sauvignon Blanc from Marlborough or Sancerre. Good with acidic and salty food. Clean and refreshing. Alternatively, try an exciting dry Manzanilla Sherry, served chilled.*

TUNA TATAKI ON MEDITERRANEAN FENNEL SALAD

SERVES 4

600g tuna loin
salt
freshly ground black pepper
2 tbsp extra virgin olive oil

Mediterranean fennel salad
1 large fennel bulb, sliced
150g semi-dried tomatoes
150g yellow cherry tomatoes
150g red cherry tomatoes
150g red capsicum, roasted
   and chopped
150g green olives
100g capers
100g red onion, sliced
¼ cup fresh basil
100ml extra virgin olive oil
45ml red wine vinegar

*Wine match: Chardonnay
from New Zealand or
Burgundy, with ripe flavours
and subtle oak, picks up the
oily richness of tuna with its
herbal accent of fennel.
Or, try a nicely chilled new-
wave dry New Zealand Rosé.*

Season the tuna loin liberally with salt and pepper and coat lightly in oil. Heat a pan big enough to take the loin in one piece. When the pan is very hot place the oiled tuna in and sear evenly on all sides. Do not cook the tuna through.

Mix together the fennel, tomatoes, capsicum, olives, capers, red onion and basil. Dress with the olive oil and red wine vinegar. Toss and mix all the flavours and juices around.

TO SERVE
Spread half of the salad on a large platter or individual plates. Slice the tuna into even rectangles and toss with the remaining salad. Build into a nice stack and dress with the remaining juices from the salad bowl.

ROAST PARMIGIANO OIL

MAKES 200ML

200g Parmigiano-Reggiano
    cheese rind
180ml grapeseed oil
1 sprig fresh rosemary

Place the Parmigiano rind and grapeseed oil in a small pot. Ensure the Parmigiano is covered by the oil. Gently bring it to a simmer and, as soon as it begins to bubble, remove it from the heat and allow to cool. Repeat this 7 times, always allowing the oil to cool completely. On the last time add the sprig of rosemary.

The oil can then be stored in a clean oil jar.

TO SERVE
This beautiful flavoured oil can now be used to drizzle over fresh pasta, to splash on a warm winter soup just before serving, as a bread dip or as a base oil when making a Caesar dressing. It is very versatile and totally delicious.

CRAYFISH OIL

MAKES 200ML

4 crayfish tail shells
60g tomato paste
200ml grapeseed oil
1 fresh rosemary sprig

Roast the crayfish tail shells at 100°C for about 2 hours until they are dry and crisp.

Transfer the dried shells to a medium saucepan and add the tomato paste. Cook the paste and shells for about 5 minutes at a medium heat to dry and cook out the tomato paste.

Add the grapeseed oil and bring the mixture just to the boil, remove from the heat and allow to cool completely. Repeat this three times.

Pass the oil through a muslin cloth and add the fresh sprig of rosemary. Store in a clean oil jar.

TO SERVE
This oil is delicious used to finish fresh seafood pastas, drizzle over hot soups, or splash over hot prawns from the barbecue. We use it with lemon juice and Dijon mustard to make a delightful dressing for seafood salads.

SPICED CHOCOLATE TRUFFLES

MAKES 20

180g dark Valrhona chocolate
75ml white port
¼ tsp vanilla extract
1tsp mild curry powder
¼ tsp five spice powder
¼ tsp ground ginger
¼ tsp ground cinnamon
25g unsalted butter, softened
cocoa powder

Wine match: *20-year-old Tawny Port (Oporto), or Liqueur Muscat from Rutherglen in North-East Victoria. Heaven!*

Chop the chocolate into small, pea-sized pieces. Heat the white port to scalding, then pour it over the chocolate and stir until you get a smooth paste. Mix in the vanilla with the spices and leave at room temperature, covered. When the chocolate mixture begins to firm up, stir in the softened butter.

Form into large, marble-sized balls and drop into the cocoa powder to coat. Store at room temperature.

TO SERVE
Accompany with coffee or after-dinner drinks.

BANANA, ALMOND AND VANILLA FRIANDS

MAKES 12

175g unsalted butter, melted
250g ground almonds
6 egg whites, lightly beaten
2 tsp vanilla extract
375g icing sugar
125g standard or cake flour
2 fresh bananas

Preheat the oven to 190°C and grease individual friand moulds.

Place all the ingredients except the bananas in a bowl and stir until combined. Half-fill each mould and top with fresh sliced banana. Bake for 25 minutes.

Paprika, thyme or cayenne, and smoked cheddar can be used as the base of canapés topped with slices of rare lamb and venison.

PARMIGIANO, ROSEMARY AND SUMAC SHORTBREADS

MAKES 30

90g Parmigiano-Reggiano
    cheese, grated
1 tbsp finely chopped
    rosemary
90g standard or cake flour
65g cold butter
1 tbsp sumac

Combine the Parmigiano, rosemary and flour in a food processor, then add the butter to form a dough. Roll the dough into a log and rest it in the refrigerator.

When you are ready to use the shortbread, preheat the oven to 190°C. Roll out the dough to a 3mm-thick sheet and sprinkle the top with the sumac. Allow to rest before cutting out the shapes.

Bake until golden.

Wine match: *Italian red from Chianti or Montepulciano d'Abruzzo. Cuts through the cheese, and refreshes the palate.*

MUSSELS STUFFED WITH A CRAYFISH MOUSSE

SERVES 4

12 greenlip mussels
2 fresh bay leaves
2 cloves garlic
100ml water

Crayfish mousse
100g crayfish meat
50g white fish
2 tbsp minced shallot
1 egg white, whisked to a
    stiff peak
1/2 cup full cream, whisked
    to a soft peak
sea salt
coarsely ground white pepper

1 tsp finely sliced red chilli
1/2 tsp finely sliced kaffir
    lime leaf
1 tsp finely sliced lemon zest
1 tbsp unsalted butter

Heat a small empty saucepan with a lid until a few drops of water run around the base as bubbles. Put the mussels into the hot pan first and leave for about 30 seconds. Stir, then add the bay leaves, garlic cloves and water and cover immediately. Cook, covered, until the mussels just begin to open. Do not overcook them as they are going to be steamed again. Remove the mussels and keep the juice. Remove the beards and shells and refrigerate the mussels.

Finely chop the crayfish and white fish, then add the shallot, egg white and cream and season with salt and pepper. Spoon or pipe the mousse into each mussel cavity.

TO SERVE
Bring 1/2 cup of the reserved mussel juice to a simmer. Add the red chilli, kaffir lime leaf and lemon zest and stir in the butter. Keep this warm.

Steam the mussels over boiling water, covered, for about 2 minutes. Serve with a spoonful of the infused juice.

Wine match: *The best and richest Chardonnay you can find – White Burgundy or the best of New Zealand. Flavours and textures are a perfect match.*

MALT VINEGAR AND BROWN SUGAR PICKLED ONIONS

MAKES 1 LITRE

400ml malt vinegar
200ml water
200g dark brown sugar
1 red chilli, split
1/2 stick cinnamon
1 star anise
1/2 tsp Szechuan peppercorns
1/2 tsp coriander seeds
2 cloves garlic
1 bay leaf
600g pickling onions, peeled

Combine the malt vinegar, water, dark brown sugar and split red chilli. Simmer to dissolve the sugar.

Lightly toast the cinnamon stick, star anise, Szechuan peppercorns and coriander seeds. Keep all of these whole and add to the pickle solution. Add the garlic and bay leaf.

With the solution at a gentle simmer, add the peeled pickling onions. This will cool the solution, so keep it on the heat and bring back to a gentle simmer. Keep it at this constant temperature for about 4 minutes. Remove from the heat and allow the onions to cool in the solution.

Store in a clean airtight container for 1 month before using.

LAVOSH SHARDS WITH ROASTED KELP SALT

SERVES 4

200g high grade or bread flour
1/2 tsp caster sugar
25g unsalted butter, softened
80ml full cream milk
30g konbu (dried kelp)
1 tbsp sea salt
1 egg
1 tbsp water

Sift the flour and caster sugar. Add the softened butter and rub in. Mix in the milk to form a smooth dough. Cover and allow to rest for 30 minutes.

To make the roasted kelp salt, bake the konbu at 180°C for 6 minutes, then grind to a coarse powder. Mix the roasted kelp with the sea salt.

Mix the egg and water. Roll out the lavosh to a 2mm-thick sheet. Brush the egg wash onto the rolled-out sheet and sprinkle with the roasted kelp salt. Cut into long, triangular-shaped shards and bake at 180°C until golden and crisp.

ROAST GARLIC, CHILLI, LIME AND GINGER PESTO

MAKES 1 CUP

½ cup garlic cloves, roasted
1 tbsp deseeded and finely
    chopped whole red chilli
2 tbsp grated lime zest
1 thumb fresh ginger, peeled
1 cup coriander leaves
1 tbsp cashew nuts, roasted
100ml peanut oil
1 tbsp sesame oil
1 tsp fish sauce
2 tsp fresh lime juice

Start by combining the roasted garlic, chilli, lime zest and ginger in a food processor. Purée until the mixture forms a smooth paste. Add the coriander leaves and roasted cashew nuts and give it a quick whizz to form a coarse paste. Finish by mixing in the liquid ingredients.

ALMOND, LEMON AND HONEY DRESSING

MAKES 300ML

100g almonds, blanched,
    roasted and coarsely chopped
3 tbsp fresh lemon thyme
60g manuka honey
    (or any fragrant honey)
60ml lemon juice
120ml extra virgin olive oil

Pound the almonds with a mortar and pestle to a chunky and coarse consistency. This creates a nice 'nutty' texture in the dressing. Add the thyme, lemon juice and honey. The manuka honey provides a distinctive, strong caramel flavour and rich amber colour. Add the extra virgin olive oil and mix well.

ROAST BUTTERNUT PUMPKIN 'CAPPUCCINO' SOUP WITH NUTMEG OIL

SERVES 6
MAKES I LITRE

Butternut soup
Ikg butternut pumpkin,
    skinned and deseeded,
    cut into cubes
50g demerara sugar
100ml Sauternes or sweet
    white dessert wine
2 cardamom pods
2 cinnamon sticks
2 cloves
750ml white chicken stock
100g onion, chopped
100g celery, chopped
100g leek, chopped
2 garlic cloves, crushed

MAKES ¹/₂ CUP

Nutmeg oil
2 whole nutmegs
I tsp curry powder
¹/₂ cinnamon stick
¹/₂ tsp cayenne pepper
¹/₂ cup grapeseed oil

Place the butternut pieces and sugar in a shallow ovenproof dish (or pan). Roast at 180°C for about 10 minutes, so the sugar and pumpkin just begin to caramelise. Transfer the roasted ingredients to a saucepan and deglaze the dish/pan with the wine. Pour the liquor into a saucepan and reduce to a syrup.

Lightly toast the cardamom, cinnamon and cloves and place in a spice bag. Then add the chicken stock and spice bag to the pan, with the onion, celery, leek and garlic and cook at a moderate heat until the pumpkin is tender enough to purée.

Discard the spice bag, and in a blender purée the soup until very smooth. (You get a better result from a blender than from a food processor.) Pass through a coarse sieve.

To make the nutmeg oil, grate the fresh nutmeg. Lightly toast each spice individually to release its own aroma. Transfer the spices to a grinder and grind to a powder. Add the oil and stir in. Place all this in a muslin bag and hang with a bowl underneath. What you catch is what you use.

TO SERVE
Heat the soup and serve in a coffee cup or small bowl. Make some milk froth as you would for coffee and spoon over the soup. Drizzle with nutmeg oil and a fresh grate of nutmeg.

Wine match: *Chardonnay, with or without oak, or possibly a very trendy Viognier from New Zealand or Australia. Creamy and spicy.*

KUMARA, COCONUT AND LEMONGRASS SOUP

SERVES 6
MAKES 1.2 LITRES

1.2kg golden kumara
   (sweet potato)
60g lemongrass stem
2 kaffir lime leaves
100g shallots
100g celery
1 clove garlic
8cm piece fresh ginger
1 tbsp grapeseed oil
1200ml water
300ml coconut cream

Garnish
1 tbsp dried coconut shavings
1 tbsp shallots, sliced and
   shallow fried
1 tsp red chilli, sliced and
   shallow fried
1/2 cup fresh coriander leaves

Cut the kumara into equal pieces, break the lemongrass with the back of a knife, crumple the lime leaves, dice the shallots and celery, smash the garlic and chop the ginger.

Sweat the lemongrass, lime leaves, shallots, celery, garlic and ginger with the oil in a saucepan until the shallots become translucent. Then add the kumara and water. Bring the mixture to the boil and simmer until the kumara is very soft.

Remove from the heat and add the coconut cream. Purée while hot and pass through a medium sieve. Discard the solids.

TO SERVE
Heat the soup and ladle it into bowls. Mix together the coconut, shallot and chilli and sprinkle on top. Garnish with fresh coriander.

Wine match: *Full-bodied and aromatic Pinot Gris from New Zealand or Alsace. Will handle the lemongrass and chilli, and match the richness of the kumara.*

LIMA BEAN, HAZELNUT AND SMOKED PAPRIKA SOUP

SERVES 6
MAKES 1.2 LITRES

300g dried lima beans
100g shallots
100g celery

Soak the lima beans overnight in enough water to cover. Slice the shallots and celery and crush the garlic. Place in a medium saucepan with the oil and sweat until translucent. Drain the beans and discard the water.

1 clove garlic
1 tbsp grapeseed oil
225ml Riesling wine
600ml water
400ml full cream
1 cinnamon stick

Garnish

$1/4$ cup hazelnuts, roasted
    and peeled
2 pinches smoked paprika
2 tbsp hazelnut oil

Wine match: *Wooded Chardonnay from Australia or New Zealand. Creamy and nutty, with hints of smoky oak.*

Add the beans to the pan. Deglaze with the white wine and reduce to a syrup. Add the water and bring to a simmer. Cook until the beans are tender and beginning to break up.

Reduce the cream, with the cinnamon stick, by 40 percent. Remove the cinnamon, add the cream to the soup mixture and purée until smooth. Pass through a coarse chinois and discard any residue solids.

TO SERVE
Reheat the soup and ladle it into bowls. Break up the hazelnuts. Sprinkle the hazelnuts and a little smoked paprika over each bowl of soup, with a drizzle of hazelnut oil.

This has all the flavours and textures of sashimi, but with a sublime twist. You can replace the snapper with almost any fish of your choice.

SESAME SEARED SNAPPER SASHIMI, PICKLED GINGER AND LOTUS ROOT SALAD

SERVES 4

400g fillet of snapper, skinned
    and boned
1 tsp grated fresh wasabi
1 tsp black sesame seeds
1 tsp sesame seeds, toasted
2 tsp soy sauce
4 tbsp pickled ginger
2 red radishes, sliced
4 cups mesclun salad
4 crispy lotus root discs, thinly
    sliced and shallow fried
4 tbsp sesame oil
2 tbsp grapeseed oil

Arrange the snapper in thin slices on the plate and give each piece a light rub with the grated wasabi. Sprinkle the snapper with some mixed sesame seeds and a light splash of soy sauce.

Arrange 4 delicate salads of pickled ginger, radish, mesclun and a lotus root garnish.

TO SERVE
Heat the sesame oil and grape seed oil to smoking. Carefully spoon the smoking oil over the raw fish on the plate. The fish will sizzle and just slightly sear and the oil will create a light sauce with the other ingredients. Serve immediately.

Wine match: *Dry Gewürztraminer from New Zealand or Alsace. Rich and spicy, long and flavoursome, with a hint of Botrytis to pick up on the ginger.*

Preparation for this recipe needs to begin a day in advance.

SAFFRON CEVICHE OF JOHN DORY AND TOMATO

SERVES 4

Ceviche base

1 pinch saffron tips
1/2 cup ponzu sauce
1 tsp soy sauce
1/3 cup mirin
2 tsp fish sauce
2 tbsp fresh lime juice
2 tbsp grated light palm sugar
400g John Dory fillet, skin removed
4 kelp salt lavosh springs (see page 50)

Salad

12 red cherry tomatoes, halved
12 yellow cherry tomatoes, halved
2 red radishes, finely sliced
1 cup fresh coriander, chopped
1/4 cup chopped fresh Vietnamese mint
1/2 cup snow peas, finely sliced

To make the ceviche marinade base, warm the saffron lightly in a pan to release the natural oils, then add the ponzu sauce, soy sauce, mirin, fish sauce and lime juice. Bring this mixture to the boil to infuse the flavours. Add the palm sugar and stir to dissolve. Remove from the heat and allow to cool completely.

Place the John Dory fillets in the cold ceviche marinade and cover. Refrigerate for 24 hours.

To make the lavosh springs, you will need to make a half recipe of the Lavosh Shards with Roasted Kelp Salt. Follow the instructions up to the final cutting stage. Cut it into 200mm x 5mm strips, then wrap these pieces around a greased wooden spoon handle, or do as we do and use small lengths of dowel. Bake at 190°C until golden and crisp. Remove from the wood while still warm and allow to cool.

To make the salad, combine the tomatoes, radishes, coriander, Vietnamese mint and snow peas.

TO SERVE

Slice the John Dory into strips and arrange on the plates. Use the marinade to toss the salad and build a nice salad in the centre of the fish. Finish with a splash of extra marinade and top with the crispy kelp salt lavosh springs.

Wine match: Dry Riesling from Australia or New Zealand or, for a special treat, a dry Vendange Tardive Riesling from Alsace. Clean fruit flavours and acidity balance the fish and garnishes.

BAKED FIGS STUFFED WITH KIKORANGI BLUE CHEESE AND WRAPPED IN PANCETTA

SERVES 4

12 fresh figs
100g Kikorangi blue cheese
   (or any creamy blue cheese)
2 tbsp full cream
freshly ground black pepper
12 strips pancetta

These are easy to prepare and are delicious as a pre-dinner nibble or with a sumptuous cheese board.

Bake the figs whole at 180°C for 8 minutes. Allow to cool. Cut a pocket in the bottom. Soften the blue cheese with the cream, season with the black pepper and pipe into the centre of the fig. Wrap each fig in a strip of pancetta.

TO SERVE
Reheat the figs slightly so the cheese is warm and soft.

Wine match: Dry Amontillado Sherry or Madeira. Old rancio aged characters and developed fruit are an excellent match for the blue cheese and the caramelised fig flavours.
If having after dinner, then use a sweeter Oloroso Sherry, or Malmsey Madeira.

SUGAR-CURED DUCK HAM, SAUTÉED HONEYDEW MELON AND CROSTINI SALAD

SERVES 4

Duck ham

4 duck breasts
$^1/_2$ cup rock salt
$^3/_4$ cup caster sugar
2 cloves garlic, finely chopped
1 tsp coarsely ground black
   peppercorns
1 tbsp fresh lemon thyme
2 star anise, toasted and
   broken
2 cinnamon sticks, toasted
   and broken
2 tbsp grated orange zest

Crostini

1 stick baguette-style French
   bread
extra virgin olive oil

Dressing

2 tbsp orange juice
2 tbsp lemon juice
6 tbsp extra virgin olive oil
sea salt
coarsely ground white pepper

1 honeydew melon
1 bunch mizuna lettuce

Trim any membrane from the duck breast and make light score marks or slashes in the fat about 5mm apart.

Mix the salt, caster sugar, garlic, black pepper, lemon thyme, star anise, cinnamon and orange zest together. Rub to totally incorporate. Rub over both sides of the duck breast, leaving a good covering. Totally cover the breast with the sugar mix and refrigerate for 48 hours.

To make the crostini, cut the baguette diagonally into long fingers about 3mm thick, drizzle with the extra virgin olive oil and bake at 120°C until dry and toasted.

Prepare the dressing by combining the orange and lemon juice with the olive oil and adjusting the seasoning.

TO SERVE

Cut the melon in half and remove all the seeds with a spoon, then cut across the melon to get half-moon shapes. You should get 8 pieces from each half. Sauté the melon in a dry hot pan so that the natural sugar of the melon begins to caramelise.

Rub off the wet sugar mix from the duck breast and slice thinly.

Mix the duck breast with the mizuna, crostini and melon and dress when serving.

Wine match: Pinot Noir from New Zealand (Martinborough or Central Otago). Has red wine characters to match with the strong flavours of duck and crostini, but light cherry fruit notes to balance the melon.

POACHED PEARS WITH GOAT CHEESE WRAPPED IN PROSCIUTTO

SERVES 4

50ml water
75ml Sauternes or sweet
    white dessert wine
1 tbsp caster sugar
1 clove
½ cinnamon stick
4 baby pears

1 goat or feta cheese
4 slices prosciutto
2 tbsp pistachio nuts
4 black pepper lavosh discs
    (see page 50)

Port glaze
100ml ruby port
½ cinnamon stick

Combine the water, Sauternes and caster sugar. Bring to a steady boil and ensure that the sugar has dissolved. Add the clove and cinnamon stick. Place the pears in the hot, spiced, poaching liquor and bring it all back to a simmer. Remove from the heat and allow to cool together so the pears absorb all the delicious flavours.

Divide the goat or feta cheese into 4 even balls. Wrap each piece with a slice of prosciutto, ensuring that the cheese is completely covered.

The small lavosh biscuit adds a much-needed peppery crunch to the dish. Follow the instructions for Lavosh Shards with Roasted Kelp Salt, replacing the kelp salt with coarsely ground black pepper and changing the shape from shards to discs.

To make the port glaze, which is used here to give a delicate balance of sweetness with spice, heat the port with the cinnamon stick in a saucepan until it is reduced by 50 percent, to the consistency of honey.

TO SERVE
Put the prosciutto-wrapped goat cheeses in a moderately heated pan so that the prosciutto becomes crisp and the cheese softens. Reheat the pears in the liquor. Serve both the pears and cheese warm to maximise the flavour. Finish with some port glaze and a sprinkle of pistachios.

Wine match: *Marlborough Sauvignon Blanc, or a Pouilly-Fumé. Flavours match the goat's cheese perfectly, and the high acid will counter the salt of the ham.*

MANUKA-SMOKED TROUT WITH TOMATO CAPER COMPOTE AND ALMOND, LEMON AND HONEY DRESSING

SERVES 4

Tomato and caper compote
1kg plum tomatoes
500ml tomato consommé
6 drops Tabasco sauce
15ml Worcestershire sauce
35g demerara sugar
480g yellow cherry tomatoes
480g red cherry tomatoes
150g salted capers, washed
fresh opal basil, basil and
    mint tips for garnish

almond, lemon and honey
    dressing (see page 52)

4 rainbow trout fillets, about
    120g each, boned
brown sugar, salt and pepper,
    to taste
2 handfuls manuka chips
    (hickory may be substituted)
fresh sprigs coriander

Wine match: *Wood-aged Chardonnay from New Zealand, Australia or Burgundy, with smoky oak flavours and richness to complement the smoked trout flavour and texture.*

For the compote, combine the plum tomatoes and consommé in a saucepan and cook slowly to a purée, stirring to ensure it does not catch on the base of the pan. Remove from the heat and pass through a coarse sieve. Discard the solids and retain the liquid. Transfer back to the original saucepan and cook until reduced to about 200ml. Pass through a fine sieve and discard the solids. Add the Tabasco and Worcestershire sauces and sugar to taste and allow to cool. Quarter the cherry tomatoes and add along with the capers. Garnish with opal basil, basil and mint leaves to serve.

Take 2 trout fillets, place a sprig of coriander between and tie together with string. Repeat with the remaining fillets. Sprinkle the trout with the brown sugar, salt and pepper. Shred the manuka chips into finger-sized strips. Two handfuls would be enough to use in an average domestic smoker and would smoke up to 10 portions of trout. Place the manuka wood chips into the smoker and place the seasoned fish on the grill above the chips. Start with a high heat to get a strong scent of manuka then turn down to allow a slow, consistent cooking with the manuka smoke. This results in a beautiful caramel colour and tender pink centres.

TO SERVE
Spoon a portion of compote into the centre of each plate. Remove the string, separate the trout into individual serving portions and place on top of the compote. Drizzle with the dressing.

The same technique is equally delicious used with chicken or salmon.

MANUKA-SMOKED LAMB RACK

Serves 4

4 lamb racks
1 cup manuka wood chips
coarsely ground white pepper
sea salt
2 tbsp brown sugar

We use fresh manuka chips gathered from around the trees; we shred these by hand into finger-sized pieces and let them dry out for about a week.

The brown sugar is needed to offset the bitterness caused by the smoking.

Season the lamb with coarsely ground white pepper, sea salt and brown sugar. Place it bone side down on a wire rack over the smoker and smoke at a moderate heat for 5 minutes. Remove it from the smoker, seal in a pan and bake for about 3 minutes at 180°C.

Wine match: *Cabernet Sauvignon and Merlot blend from New Zealand, Australia or the Haut-Médoc in Bordeaux. Wood-aged to match the smoked flavour, and the fruitiness goes very well with lamb.*

PASTA DOUGH

MAKES 750G

Basic pasta dough

2 eggs

4 egg yolks

20ml olive oil

2 cups high grade or
    bread flour

I cup durum wheat flour

Combine the eggs, yolks and olive oil. Sift the high grade flour into the durum wheat flour and slowly mix into the egg mixture to form a smooth dough. Allow to rest for an hour and roll when ready.

Beetroot pasta dough

I egg

4 egg yolks

20ml olive oil

20ml beetroot juice

2 cups high grade or
    bread flour

I cup durum wheat flour

Combine the egg, yolks, olive oil and beetroot juice. Sift the high grade flour into the durum wheat flour and slowly mix into the egg mixture to form a smooth dough. Cover and refrigerate. Roll out when needed.

Saffron pasta dough

I pinch saffron threads

50ml water

2 eggs

4 egg yolks

20ml olive oil

2 cups high grade or
    bread flour

I cup durum wheat flour

Heat the saffron threads and cover with the water. Reduce to a strong syrup of about 15ml. Combine the eggs, yolks, olive oil and saffron syrup. Sift the high grade flour into the durum wheat flour and slowly mix into the egg mixture to form a smooth dough. Cover and refrigerate. Roll out when needed.

SAGE PAPPARDELLE OF RABBIT, PANCETTA, PEAS, BROCCOLI, BROAD BEANS AND PECORINO CHEESE

SERVES 4

1 recipe basic Pasta Dough
    (see page 72)
¼ cup fresh sage leaves
1 cup brown chicken stock
1 cup bite-sized pieces roasted
    rabbit meat
4 tbsp peas
1 cup broccoli florets
4 tbsp broad beans, peeled
½ cup chopped pancetta
½ cup pecorino cheese
    shavings
coarsely ground black pepper

Make 1 recipe of the basic pasta dough. When it is being rolled out, on the final turn, sprinkle half the sage leaves over the pasta and double the dough over, so that the sage leaves are now between 2 sheets of pasta. Roll through the pasta machine again and cut into 2.5cm-thick strands. Allow the pappardelle to dry over a coat hanger or rolling pin for 1 hour.

Cook the pasta until *al dente*. Heat the chicken stock with the rabbit in it. Once the pasta is out of the water, cook the peas, broccoli and broad beans quickly.

Meanwhile, cut the pancetta into 2.5cm-long batons.

TO SERVE
Toss the cooked pasta, raw pancetta and cooked vegetables together. Divide amongst 4 plates. Pour the chicken stock and rabbit over and top with the remaining sage, pecorino cheese and black pepper.

Wine match: *Spicy Shiraz from Australia or the Northern Rhône. Rich and peppery, spicy flavours with warmth and length.*

RAVIOLI OF LAMB NECK, CINNAMON CELERIAC, BABY CARROTS AND GARLIC CHIPS

SERVES 4

Ravioli

1 recipe Saffron Pasta Dough
   (see page 72)
1 cup cooked and shredded
   lamb neck meat,
2 egg yolks
flour for dusting

Cinnamon celeriac purée

2 cinnamon sticks
2 large celeriac, peeled
   and diced
2 cups full cream milk
1 muslin sheet, pillowcase size

Garlic chips

4 cloves garlic
1/2 cup full cream milk

Garnish

12 baby carrots, cooked
2 tbsp lemon zest
2 tbsp fresh Italian parsley

Roll the pasta dough out to about 2mm thick sheets. Allow the dough time to rest before cutting out the discs. Cut 24 discs with a diameter of 6cm. Lay out 12 discs and spoon the lamb neck meat into the centre of each disc. Brush the edges with egg yolk and press the second pasta disc on top. Dust with a little flour and refrigerate.

To make the celeriac purée, combine the cinnamon, celeriac and milk in a medium-sized pot. Cook until the celeriac is very soft and tender. Purée in a blender. Pour onto a sheet of muslin and bring the corners up to form a hanging ball. Use a bowl to catch the liquid. Leave this to hang for at least 2 hours and you will be left with a smooth, white, speckled celeriac purée.

For the garlic chips, slice the garlic as thinly as possible, poach in the milk and refresh in water twice. Then shallow-fry in a pan at a low heat until crisp.

TO SERVE
Cook the ravioli in salted boiling water and heat the celeriac purée. Put the drained ravioli into a serving dish, pour the celeriac purée over and surround with the baby carrots. Serve with a generous sprinkling of garlic chips, lemon zest and parsley.

Wine match: New Zealand Pinot Noir, or New Zealand Syrah from Hawke's Bay. The spicy fruit of the wine will match the cinnamon, and the cool-climate style of red wine goes well with lamb ravioli.

RISOTTO OF MUSSELS, KALAMATA OLIVES, BABY FENNEL, AND GURNARD WITH TOMATO AND THYME VINAIGRETTE

SERVES 4

Tomato and thyme vinaigrette

2 plum tomatoes, skin and
    seeds removed
2 tbsp fresh lemon thyme tips
2 tbsp Chardonnay vinegar
3 tbsp avocado oil
1 tsp light palm sugar

Risotto base

2 tbsp unsalted butter
2 tbsp sliced brown onion
1 tsp garlic, chopped
1 cup carnaroli rice
4 tbsp white wine
2 cups white chicken stock
2 tbsp finely grated
    Parmigiano-Reggiano cheese
60g unsalted cold butter,
    cut into blocks

12 greenlip mussels, cooked
2 tbsp kalamata olives, slivered
4 boneless gurnard fillet
4 baby fennel bulbs

Prepare the vinaigrette first. Chop the tomatoes into small dice and combine with the lemon thyme, vinegar, oil and sugar.

To prepare the risotto base, begin by putting the first measure of butter, onion and garlic into a medium-sized saucepan. Always use a wooden spoon when preparing risotto. Cook until the onion becomes translucent. Add the rice and cook until it is warm on the back of your knuckles; this allows the outer husk to split. While constantly stirring, pour in the white wine and allow the rice to absorb it. Adding a little at a time, pour in the chicken stock, continue to stir and cook the rice until *al dente*. Mix in the Parmigiano cheese and cold butter blocks and cover. This allows the starch in the rice to settle and become creamy.

TO SERVE

Mix the mussels and olive slivers into the creamy risotto base. Pan-fry the gurnard fillet and char-grill the baby fennel. Once the risotto, gurnard and fennel are plated, spoon the tomato and thyme vinaigrette over and serve.

Wine match: Sauvignon Blanc from New Zealand, especially Marlborough, goes particularly well with this shellfish and all its condiments.

HOISIN BEEF AND SALAD WONTON STACK WITH PALM-SUGARED PEANUTS

SERVES 4

400g ginger-aged beef fillet
  (see opposite)
4 tbsp hoisin sauce
12 wonton sheets, deep fried
  until crisp

Palm-sugared peanuts

$1/2$ cup peanuts, coarsely
  crushed
4 tbsp grated light palm sugar
I pinch ground cinnamon

Dressing

5 tbsp kecap manis
2 tbsp freshly squeezed
  lime juice

Salad

I fresh red chilli, sliced and
  shallow fried until crisp
4 tbsp sliced shallot, shallow
  fried until golden
$1/4$ cup fresh mint
$1/4$ cup snow pea sprouts
$1/2$ cup fresh coriander
2 tbsp sliced spring onion
$1/2$ telegraph cucumber, cut
  into batons

Evenly sear the beef fillet in a whole piece. Cook at 180°C for 8 minutes, turning once. Remove and coat in hoisin sauce, wrap in cling film and refrigerate.

Lightly toast the peanuts and allow to cool. Then gently warm and melt the palm sugar and cinnamon, add the cold peanuts and turn with a spoon so the sugar crystallises and turns pale golden and coats the peanuts. Remove and cool ready to be used.

Mix the kecap manis and lime juice for the dressing.

TO SERVE

Combine all ingredients for the salad in a large bowl. Add a little dressing and lightly toss together to coat each piece.

Slice the cooked marinated beef into 1cm-thick slices and coat lightly in dressing.

Begin to make a stack with the crisp wontons. Ensure that you have an even mix of salad and beef in each layer. Drizzle the remaining dressing over and sprinkle with the palm-sugared peanuts.

Wine match: Merlot from New Zealand (Kumeu or Hawke's Bay), or perhaps a St. Emilion or Pomerol. Strongly flavoured beef needs a full-bodied red, but one with subtlety and elegance so the salad is not dominated.

Ginger-aged beef fillet

SERVES 4

1 fillet of beef
1 muslin cloth
150ml ginger beer
cotton string

Ask your butcher to trim the fillet or do it yourself. Remove the chine and most of the membrane. Keep the fillet whole.

Cut a piece of muslin about 10cm longer than the fillet. Soak the muslin cloth in the ginger beer. Tightly wrap the fillet like a sock in the soaked muslin cloth and tie with the string. Hang the fillet vertically in the refrigerator with the tail end at the base and a tray underneath to catch any blood. After 7 days wipe the meat with a clean damp cloth and cut into steaks to grill, or leave whole and oven roast for 20 minutes.

This method allows the enzymes to break down and soften the fillet, while the flavour of the ginger beer is absorbed and the preservatives in the ginger beer prevent any bacteria from forming.

MARINATED SALMON ESCABÈCHE WITH A WHITE GINGER SALAD

SERVES 4

Escabèche marinade
160ml extra virgin olive oil
20ml sesame oil
80ml malt vinegar
40ml Chardonnay vinegar
100ml soy sauce
1 tsp coriander seeds, toasted
1 tsp pink peppercorns, toasted
1 pinch saffron, warmed
1 tbsp ginger, chopped
1 shallot, cut into rings

4 x 120g salmon fillet portions
1 carrot, finely sliced
1 celeriac, finely sliced
2 tbsp pickled white ginger
2 tbsp peanuts, roasted
2 kaffir lime leaves, finely sliced
1 spring onion, sliced
   diagonally into 'diamonds'
2 tsp grated fresh ginger

Combine the oils, vinegars and soy sauce. Lightly pound the toasted coriander seeds and pink peppercorns and add with the warmed saffron to the liquid mixture. Mix in the ginger and shallot.

Place the salmon in the marinade, and add the carrot and celeriac to cover the salmon. Leave to marinate for 24 hours.

Remove the salmon from the marinade and sauté on its skin side for approximately 2 minutes only. Take care as the salmon will darken very quickly. This is a very delicate dish that is best eaten pink. Combine the pickled ginger, roasted peanuts, kaffir lime leaves, spring onion, carrot and celeriac into 4 balls.

TO SERVE
Place the salad ball on the plate first, then lean the salmon up against it as well as a small ball of freshly grated ginger. Spoon some marinade over and serve.

Wine match: *Wood-aged New Zealand Chardonnay or White Burgundy to match the richness and texture of salmon and to complement the spicy ginger.*

POACHED TAMARILLOS, PALM SUGAR MERINGUE AND PASSIONFRUIT

SERVES 4

Poached tamarillos
1 vanilla bean, split
1 whole clove
1 tsp ground allspice
4 tbsp light brown sugar
1 cup water
12 baby tamarillos, peeled

Palm sugar meringue
220g light palm sugar, grated
2½ tbsp liquid glucose
80ml water
6 egg whites

4 fresh passionfruit
4 tbsp passionfruit syrup

Wine match: *Tropical fruit characters and high acidity from the tamarillos will go very well with a Sauternes (Bordeaux) or Botrytis-style Sémillon from Australia or New Zealand.*

Mix the vanilla bean, clove, allspice, light brown sugar and water together and bring this to a simmer to dissolve the sugar. Add the peeled tamarillos to the hot solution. Remove from the heat and allow to cool, covered. This allows the tamarillos to absorb all the beautiful spices.

To make the meringue, mix the palm sugar, glucose and water and heat to 110°C using a sugar thermometer. Whisk the egg whites to a stiff peak. Slowly pour in the hot sugar and whisk until cool.

Mix the fresh passionfruit with the passionfruit syrup.

TO SERVE
Spoon the soft meringue onto a plate. Place the slightly warmed tamarillos on top. Drizzle with passionfruit syrup.

HOT CHOCOLATE FONDANT

SERVES 4

135g Valrhona Guanaja
   chocolate
100g unsalted butter
14g cornflour
170g caster sugar
2 whole eggs
2 egg yolks
1 tsp Grand Marnier liqueur

Wine match: *Liqueur Tokay or Muscat from Rutherglen, or try it with a shot of Grand Marnier.*

Melt the chocolate and butter until soft and combined. Mix together the cornflour and caster sugar. Stir this into the chocolate mixture to form a smooth but grainy paste. Allow to cool slightly. Whisk the eggs and liqueur together to break up the yolks, and stir this in to finish the batter.

Preheat the oven to 190°C. Line 4 baking rings with greaseproof paper and fill each with a quarter of the mixture. Bake for 12 minutes and serve immediately.

TO SERVE
We serve this delicious recipe with several combinations. One that goes very well with it is Rhubarb and Clove Ice Cream (see page 92).

ROAST PINEAPPLE, SAKE AND STAR ANISE NECTAR

MAKES 1 LITRE

2 pineapples
120ml sake
2 star anise
1 cinnamon stick
2 tbsp demerara sugar
500ml pineapple juice
2 tbsp fresh lime juice

Peel and core the pineapples, then cut into quarters. Combine the sake, star anise, cinnamon and sugar. Pour over the pineapple and allow to macerate for 24 hours.

Place in a shallow baking pan and bake at 180°C, basting regularly, until the pineapple begins to caramelise at the edges. Remove and purée everything. Pass through a coarse sieve.

Finish with the lime juice to taste. Being nectar it should be slightly thick and pulpy.

TO SERVE
Serve it in a frozen shot glass with a pineapple wafer, made by drying out thin slices of pineapple in a slow oven for an hour.

Preparation for this recipe needs to begin a day in advance.

FROMAGE BLANC WITH STRAWBERRIES AND PISTACHIO CARAMEL

SERVES 4

Fromage blanc
60g mascarpone
40g crème fraîche
1 vanilla bean, split and
    seeds scraped out
50g caster sugar
100ml thickened cream
50g sweetened yoghurt
4 pieces muslin cloth,
    each about 25cm square

Pistachio caramel
1/4 cup caster sugar
1 drop lemon juice
2 tbsp water
70g shelled pistachio nuts

Strawberries
1/4 vanilla bean
1 tbsp lime juice
40g caster sugar
40ml water
1 punnet fresh strawberries,
    washed and quartered

8 fresh mint tips
12 fresh basil tips

Combine the mascarpone, crème fraîche, vanilla bean seeds and sugar. Fold through the thickened cream and yoghurt. Divide evenly into 4 portions and spoon into the muslin squares. Bring the corners of the muslin together, forming the balls of fromage blanc. Hang these in the refrigerator overnight to firm up, with a tray below to catch any drips.

The pistachio caramel needs to be made in advance. Mix the caster sugar, lemon juice and water together. Cook to a golden caramel. Add the pistachios and pour onto greaseproof paper in long, thin finger swirls. Allow to cool, then break up and pile into 4 bundles.

For the strawberries, mix the vanilla, lime juice, caster sugar and water together. Bring to the boil to dissolve the sugar. Allow to cool totally, then add the fresh strawberries to marinate for 1 hour before serving.

TO SERVE
Place the marinated strawberries on serving plates and arrange the mint and basil tips around them. Carefully turn the fromage blanc out of the muslin and set on the strawberries. Top with pistachio caramel.

Wine match: *Late harvest Riesling from New Zealand or Australia or, for something completely different, a sweet sparkling Moscato from Asti.*

RHUBARB AND CLOVE ICE CREAM

MAKES 1 LITRE

430ml full cream milk
430ml full cream
2 vanilla beans, split
10 egg yolks
150g caster sugar
300g rhubarb stalks, peeled
    but reserve the skin
1 tsp rosewater
100ml water
100g caster sugar
4 whole cloves
2 star anise
1 cinnamon stick
1 tbsp grenadine

Wine match: *Serve with very sweet Sherry, Pedro Ximenes or Moscato.*

Begin by mixing the milk, cream and vanilla beans together. (Keep the empty vanilla pods to combine with some caster sugar and in a couple of days you will have some great vanilla sugar.) Bring the cream mixture to a simmer. Whisk the egg yolks and caster sugar to combine. Pour the hot cream mixture over the yolks a little at a time, whisking to incorporate. Return this mixture to a moderate heat and cook until the mixture coats the back of a spoon. Pass through a fine sieve and allow to cool.

Chop the rhubarb into short lengths, and add the rosewater, water and caster sugar. Place the reserved skin in a spice bag with the cloves, star anise and cinnamon stick. Cook over a moderate heat until the rhubarb is mushy, falling apart, and the liquid has reduced by three-quarters. Remove the spice bag and allow to cool.

Mix the cold rhubarb with the ice cream base, add the grenadine and churn in an ice cream machine. Store in the freezer ready for serving.

This ice cream has a delicious twist on some classical flavours.

TERRINE OF LEMON, THYME AND HONEYCOMB ICE CREAM

MAKES 1 LITRE

Ice cream base
430ml full cream milk
430ml cream
2 vanilla beans, split
150g caster sugar
10 egg yolks

Honeycomb
130g caster sugar
1 tbsp manuka honey
   (or any fragrant honey)
2 tbsp liquid glucose
1 tbsp water
1/3 tsp bicarbonate of soda

4 tbsp grated lemon zest
2 tbsp fresh lemon thyme tips

Wine match: *Late Harvest or Botrytis Riesling from New Zealand or Australia. The lemon aroma and intense fruit sweetness combine well with the ice cream flavours. Alternatively, late harvest Riesling from Germany or Austria, or a classic 6 Puttonyos Tokaj from Hungary.*

Begin by mixing the milk, cream and vanilla beans together. Bring this to a simmer. Whisk the caster sugar and yolks to combine. Pour the hot cream mix over the yolks a little at a time, whisking to incorporate. Return this mixture to a moderate heat and cook until the mixture coats the back of a spoon. Pass through a fine sieve and allow to cool.

Make the honeycomb in a large saucepan as the mix doubles in size. Lay an A4-sized sheet of baking paper out on the bench.

Mix together the caster sugar, honey, glucose and water. Cook over a moderate heat until it becomes golden brown. Add the bicarbonate of soda and whisk quickly. At this stage the mix will grow in size dramatically and turn into a molten-lava consistency. Pour out onto the prepared baking paper and allow to cool. When the honeycomb has cooled, break it up into little bite-sized nuggets.

Add the lemon zest and lemon thyme tips to the cooled ice cream base and churn. When the ice cream is ready add two-thirds of the honeycomb and churn just to mix in. Remove from the machine and freeze in a terrine mould.

TO SERVE
Slice and sprinkle with the reserved honeycomb.
The terrine will keep for up to 2 weeks in the freezer.

GLOSSARY

Blini pan – special pan for making blini, small Russian yeast pancakes.

Blood oranges – *Citrus sinensis*, sweet, juicy orange variety with red flesh, eaten fresh or used in salads.

Bocconcini – (Italian) small balls of fresh white cheese similar to mozzarella.

Celeriac – knobbly brown vegetable, the root of a special celery that tastes like a cross between a strong celery and parsley.

Ceviche – (Latin American) fresh raw fish marinated in lime and seasonings.

Chinois – fine mesh metal cone-shaped sieve used for sieving sauces and purées.

Crème fraîche – sharp-flavoured velvety matured sour cream.

Deglaze – add a small amount of liquid, usually wine or stock, to the pan after meat or other food is cooked to use as a base for a sauce.

Durum flour – hard wheat flour with high gluten content, used for making pasta.

Escabèche – (Spanish) a dish of poached or fried fish, covered with a spicy marinade and chilled.

Flour – standard or cake flour is a soft flour; high grade or bread flour is a strong flour.

Grapeseed oil – light, fragrant oil extracted from grape seeds. Used for salad dressings and also for sautéing because it has a high smoke point.

Grenadine – sweet, deep red, pomegranate-flavoured syrup used to colour and flavour drinks and desserts.

Kaffir lime leaves – from the kaffir lime tree, used in Asian cooking. Available fresh or dried, but fresh leaves have a more intense, fragrant aroma.

Kecap manis – (Indonesian) also called ketjap manis. A syrupy, dark brown sauce similar to soy sauce but sweeter.

Mascarpone – (Italian) a buttery-rich cream cheese made from cow's milk, used in sweet and savoury dishes.

Mesclun salad – (French) selection of small, young, slightly bitter salad greens.

Mirin – (Japanese) sweet rice wine used in cooking.

Mizuna lettuce – (Japanese) feathery, delicate salad green.

Pancetta – (Italian) flavoursome bacon cured with salt and spices but not smoked.

Pappardelle – (Italian) wide noodles with rippled sides.

Parmigiano-Reggiano – Italian Parmesan cheese made from cow's milk. A hard, granular cheese with a thick rind, and relatively low in fat.

Pecorino cheese – (Italian) hard, granular cheese made from sheep's milk.

Ponzu – (Japanese) sauce made with lemon juice or vinegar, soy sauce, rice wine, konbu seaweed and dried bonito flakes.

Portobello mushrooms – large, well-flavoured, dark brown mushrooms with an open, flat cap and meaty texture.

Prosciutto – (Italian) ham that has been seasoned, salt-cured (but not smoked) and air-dried.

Roma tomatoes – (Italian) a plum tomato variety, oval-shaped with few seeds and ideal for Italian tomato sauces.

Salmon caviar – also called red caviar. Medium-sized, orange to red salmon eggs with a fresh salty flavour, less expensive than true caviar (eggs of the female sturgeon).

Sausage skin – available from butchers' shops.

Star anise – (Asian) star-shaped, dark brown pod with a seed in each of its eight segments and a slightly bitter aniseed flavour.

Sumac – (Middle Eastern) dark purple-red berries sold dried or ground with a fruity, astringent taste. Used in fish, meat and vegetables dishes.

Szechuan peppercorns – (Chinese) dried red-brown berries used ground to add fragrant spiciness to dishes.

Tamarillo – *Cyphomandra betacea*, also called tree tomato. Deep red or orange egg-shaped, slightly tart fruit.

Tomato consommé – clear, flavoursome tomato stock. Can be purchased in Tetra Paks.

Tomato paste – concentrated paste made from tomatoes reduced to about one-fifth of their original weight.

Valrhona chocolate – high-quality dark chocolate available from delicatessens. Valrhona Guanaja is a dark, bitter chocolate with a higher percentage of cacao.

Verjuice – (French) lightly acidic unfermented grape juice used instead of vinegar in cooking.

INDEX